The Roth Window
A Retirement Strategy for the Tax Reform Era

By
Gene R. Ric
and
Mike Due

Preface

Here's the main message of this book, right up front, offered on the first page so you don't really need to read the rest of this book. I've got the silver bullet loaded, and ready to shoot this nugget of knowledge with no further delays:

> **Right now, and for a (likely) limited number of years ahead, there's a significant advantage in using the ROTH IRA to save for your retirement, which will leverage tax changes and compound interest to put more equity into your retirement bunker than ever before.**

That's the main idea. Turn out the light, good night, sleep well. In the morning, pick up a Roth right after stopping for coffee and you are on your way to building wealth. Thanks for reading.

Ah, we knew you'd keep reading, for some reason. Perhaps you want to know why this is true? Or maybe you want to know more details or see some proof of this financial planning super strategy. You are right to want to know more. So, turn that light back on, get jacked up on a late-night espresso, and read on.

About the Authors

Mike Due is a writer living in Cincinnati, OH. He is here only for his writing abilities and publishing knowledge. The real brainpower is coming from the next guy, Gene.

Gene R. Ric is a financial professional who works for one of the largest investment houses in the country. As a *Covered Person* in the financial services industry, any digital or written communication he produces is subject to review by his employer, which would almost certainly take too much time for approval and may be denied in the end. Therefore, Gene R. Ric (which is not his real name, and only a play on the word 'generic') has chosen to forego all compensation and let Mike Due bring this strategy to you instead. The reason for this arrangement is so he could deliver this information to you in a timely manner. If he had gone any other route, some of this subject's timeliness/usefulness would be lost. Mike Due is just a ghost writer for Gene R. Ric. So why should you take financial advice from someone who won't go by his real name? You should not. You should only take financial advice from a trusted professional. Our hope, here, is that you will read this book and share the ideas with your advisors... and then you can trust them. And, we believe Gene's ideas stand on their own, regardless of the person bringing them to you.

Who is This Book For?

We should tell you, this strategy, which we are calling the **Roth Window**, is much more applicable to certain investors than others. You'll need to read on to see if this strategy applies to you or consult your own investment professionals to discuss this strategy's applicability to you and your family. Read on, and we'll discuss this in more detail, but just know for the time being, it's not a one-size-fits-all retirement savings strategy. The idea is a simple one, but how it plugs into your financial profile will take some tweaking.

Indeed, it takes money to make money, and the Roth Window strategy is no exception. **This is not a strategy for someone starting to save for retirement from scratch**. If you have significant pre-tax retirement assets or expect to have significant pre-tax retirement assets by the age of 70, then you may benefit from this strategy. If you are under the age of 65, this book may provide strategies for building long-term wealth. If you are a highly compensated employee, there may be an opportunity to accelerate tax-free savings beyond the imposed limits of contributions into an IRA or employer retirement savings plan. The Roth Window presents a strategy to save tens of thousands of dollars — and for some, hundreds of thousands of dollars — in taxes over the lifetime of the assets. If you are a tax advisor or financial planner, you need to understand how this opportunity may benefit your clients.

Why Now?

You may be wondering... the Roth IRA, as a retirement vehicle, is not new. It was legislated into existence by lawmakers back in 1997 (https://en.wikipedia.org/wiki/Roth_IRA#History). So why are Mike and Gene writing this book now, and why is this Roth Window a timely consideration? That's a great question. The answer is directly tied to the changes in the *Tax Cuts & Jobs Act* of 2018. These changes have created an opportunity not previously available to investors. Unfortunately, that legislation may expire in less than a decade, closing a window of opportunity that exists only between 2018 and 2026. That's why we're calling this strategy the **Roth Window**, and that's why you should keep reading.

Disclaimer

As stated earlier, **the information in this book should not be consider financial or tax advice.** Rather, the ideas found here are a good conversation starter for you and your financial advisor. The goal of this book is to help you understand a potential strategy that may or may not apply to your unique circumstance. Everyone's situation is unique, and we encourage you to consult with a professional before applying this, or any other investment strategy. **This strategy does not account for state taxes, so if you live in a state with high income tax rates, this may not be as beneficial based on your situation.**

Chapter 1 - Roth Window

The Tax Cuts & Jobs Act of 2018, signed into law by President Trump, has created significant changes to our tax laws, by reducing marginal tax rates, adjusting tax brackets, and doubling the standard deduction, for starters. Everyone's excited that they get to keep a little more of their money in their paychecks. But what some may not know, is that these tax rates, unless extended by Congress, are scheduled to expire on December 31, 2025 and revert to 2017 tax rates. So, for now, it looks like we're only going to benefit from this legislation for eight years! As a result, we have an eight-year window of opportunity to take advantage of the lowest tax rates we have seen it decades. In 2017, a couple filing Joint with $85,000 in taxable income, were in a 25% tax bracket. In 2018, a couple filing Joint with $315,000 in taxable income, are in a 24% tax bracket. Why is this important? Roth Conversions! The benefits of a Roth are well documented, and we will discuss them in detail later. We have all heard, "the two things you cannot escape are death and taxes." Not to mention higher gas prices during the summer months. But We digress. Indeed, you cannot avoid paying taxes, but you do have choices about **when** you pay them. That's important, because the timing of paying taxes will alter how your wealth accumulates over time. This will be revisited shortly, here, as it is an important component of the Roth Window concept.

There are different types of dollars in retirement savings accounts. It is extremely important to understand the different types of dollars and how you can leverage these dollars to build wealth. There are three types of dollars: Pre-tax dollars, After-tax dollars, and Roth dollars. These types of dollars can be in an employer retirement savings plan (401k, 403b, 401a) or an Individual Retirement Account (IRA).

- **Pre-tax dollars** have never been taxed. They can come into a retirement savings plan through payroll deduction and/or company matching/discretionary contributions, or they can be After-tax dollars that are contributed to an IRA and then turned into pre-tax dollars by taking a tax deduction on your tax return.

- **After-tax dollars** have been taxed. It is less common to see these types of dollars in a retirement savings plan, but if you are highly compensated, it represents a significant opportunity. Within a retirement savings plan, as these after-tax dollars gain in value, the profit is pre-tax dollars, so at some point when the profit is withdrawn, you will have to pay taxes on the profit that your After-tax dollars generated.

- **Roth dollars** are magical. Roth dollars in a retirement savings plan have already been taxed, like After-tax dollars. The difference is that as these dollars grow, the profit is tax-free. Over long periods of time, this can be a very powerful tool in building wealth. The trick, and this book, are about turning your dollars into magical Roth dollars.

For years, financial advisors have debated which retirement account is better, a pre-tax retirement savings account or a Roth retirement savings account. Let's weigh the pros and cons of both approaches.

- **A pre-tax retirement account***, provides a reduction in your taxable income, giving you more money to spend in the year you contribute to a retirement plan. But down the road, you'll have to pay taxes on that money.
  * Rollover IRA, Traditional IRA, SEP IRA, Simple IRA, 401k, 403b, 401a, or 457.

- **A Roth**, on the other hand, is funded with dollars that have been taxed. You pay Uncle Sam taxes on the money prior to contributing, and then the Roth grows tax-free over the years and all moneys withdrawn from the Roth (once you meet certain requirements) are tax-free.

What it boils down to is this: Should you pay taxes on your investment money now, or later? Many advisors have suggested that having a mix of these two options is best for investors. And perhaps that is true under normal circumstances. But now, and for the next eight years, we believe that contributing dollars to a Roth, or converting pre-tax dollars to Roth is the best strategy, and if possible, having 100% of your retirement asset in a tax-free retirement savings plan will provide the greatest control of income and wealth in retirement.

We contend, under the new tax laws, the opportunity exists for the average wage-earner to prepay taxes at a lower effective tax rate on large portions of their pre-tax retirement savings to position assets for tax-free growth. An average family, filing jointly, may be able to convert $100,000 to $150,000 each year for the next 8 years. Since there are no RMDs (Required Minimum Distributions, discussed later) during the lifetime of the Roth assets, the money grows tax-free for the rest of your life time and the lifetime of your heirs. This could be 40 to 50 years of tax-free growth.

Of course, there's always a chance that in eight-year, congress will extend the lower tax rates. If they allow them to expire, and return to higher tax rates, this Roth Window will be slammed shut. That's why taking advantage of the lower taxes NOW is so important. Nobody has a crystal ball to know what will happen, but as of today, these tax rates do have a limited life expectancy.

When considering taxes, we tend to look for ways to save taxes on a year-to-year basis. Consider paying more taxes, at a lower effective tax rate today, rather than paying higher taxes after December 31, 2025 on a larger pre-tax account as it grows. Below, we will model several different scenarios to illustrate the benefits of this strategy and how it can save you tens-of-thousands of dollars over the life of your assets.

How about an example? Examples are good, right? This will give us a way to see how the Roth Window concept could impact a real person's growth of retirement funds.

Example #1

Mr. and Mrs. Penny are 60 years old and have a joint income of $80,000 per year. They plan to retire at the full retirement age of 67 at which time they expect their annual income to be reduced to $50,000 per year which would include social security, pension and an annuity. As far as what they've saved for retirement, they have a combination of 401k's and pre-tax Rollover IRA's totaling $500,000 and an after-tax brokerage account worth $88,000. The question is, should they just do nothing, and let those existing retirement vehicles do their job? Or should they do something differently?

Option A: They do nothing.

Assuming they do not withdraw any of the money, and assuming those investments will produce a meager 6% rate of return (which is a pretty conservative assumption, and could be higher), their pre-tax assets will be worth $894,000 at age 70, when the government tells them they must start receiving cash from the investments as RMDs, (Required Minimum Distributions). At that time, it will be 2028 and the favorable tax rates associated with the Tax Cuts & Jobs Act of 2018 will (quite possibly) have expired.

Option B: They could choose to convert $85,000 per year for each of the next seven years to a ROTH IRA.

By the time they reach the end of that seven-year period, they will have converted all their pre-tax assets. Because they want to pay taxes up front when converting money into the ROTH, they decide to use the $88,000 in their brokerage account to pay those taxes.

Wow, that's gotta hurt... taking $85,000 out of a retirement account and paying Uncle Sam tax ($14,516 per year) on that money now, especially thinking you could alternatively wait to pay that down the road, right? But the way this shakes out, it will be more beneficial to pay the taxes now instead of later.

If the Penny family chose Option B, they would reach a breakeven point within 5 years, around age 65. This means the value of Option A's investments would be approximately equal to the value of Option B's investment. Then, moving into the next five years, Option B will really begin to shine brightly, as that money will continue to grow tax-free. The taxes had already been paid, remember? So, by age 70, (Option B) the tax-free Roth account and after-tax account combined will be worth about $87,800 **more** than the pre-tax retirement & after-tax brokerage accounts combined (Option A).

And it only gets better moving into retirement. By age 85, which is 25 years after the conversion began, the Roth retirement account would be worth **almost $250,000 more** than the pre-tax and taxable accounts combined (option A). The best part is that the Roth assets will continue to grow tax-free for Mr. and Mrs. Penny's heirs (under the Roth retirement account) whereas the pre-tax retirement account will be forced out due to RMDs (Required Minimum Distributions) and at best, reinvested in a taxable brokerage account.

So how about an illustration? Illustrations are good, right?

Case Study Assumptions:

Age in 2018	60
Estimated age of retirement	67
Filing Status	Married Filing Joint
Per tax assets in 2018	$500,000.00
After Tax assets in 2018	$88,000.00
Assume Investment rate of return	6%
Current Income	$80,000.00
Estimated income in Retirement	$50,000.00
Investment Income Tax rate, Assumed LTCG	15%
Tax rate for Net Total Combined	18%

Model assumes RMD's are taken on Janurary 1st of each year, After-tax profit subject to LTCG rate

Option 1: Do nothing

Year	Age	Pre tax Assets	IRS Uniform Lifetime Tax Table	RMD	Effective Tax Rate	Less Taxes	Reinvested in Taxable Acct Jan 1st	Profit	Taxes on LTCG Dec 31st	Taxable Acct Total Per Year	Net Total Combined
2018	60	$500,000.00								$88,000.00	$498,000.00
2019	61	$530,000.00						$5,280.00	$792.00	$92,488.00	$527,088.00
2020	62	$561,800.00						$5,549.28	$832.39	$97,204.89	$557,880.89
2021	63	$595,508.00						$5,832.29	$874.84	$102,162.34	$590,478.90
2022	64	$631,238.48						$6,129.74	$919.46	$107,372.62	$624,988.17
2023	65	$669,112.79						$6,442.36	$966.35	$112,848.62	$661,521.11
2024	66	$709,259.56						$6,770.92	$1,015.64	$118,603.90	$700,196.74
2025	67	$751,815.13						$7,116.23	$1,067.44	$124,652.70	$741,141.10
2026	68	$796,924.04						$7,479.16	$1,121.87	$131,009.99	$784,487.70
2027	69	$844,739.48						$7,860.60	$1,179.09	$137,691.50	$830,377.87
2028	70	$895,423.85	$27.40	$32,679.70	$0.15	$4,801.29	$27,878.41	$9,934.19	$1,490.13	$174,013.97	$908,261.53
2029	71	$914,508.79	$26.50	$34,509.77	$0.15	$5,147.20	$29,362.57	$12,202.59	$1,830.39	$213,748.74	$963,645.96
2030	72	$932,798.97	$25.60	$36,437.46	$0.15	$5,516.67	$30,920.79	$14,680.17	$2,202.03	$257,147.68	$1,022,042.84
2031	73	$950,143.20	$24.70	$38,467.34	$0.15	$5,911.02	$32,556.32	$17,382.24	$2,607.34	$304,478.91	$1,083,596.33
2032	74	$966,376.42	$23.80	$40,604.05	$0.16	$6,331.60	$34,272.45	$20,325.08	$3,048.76	$356,027.67	$1,148,456.34
2033	75	$981,318.71	$22.90	$42,852.35	$0.16	$6,779.79	$36,072.55	$23,526.01	$3,528.90	$412,097.34	$1,216,778.68
2034	76	$994,774.34	$22.00	$45,217.02	$0.16	$7,256.99	$37,960.03	$27,003.44	$4,050.52	$473,010.29	$1,288,725.26
2035	77	$1,006,530.77	$21.20	$47,477.87	$0.16	$7,718.40	$39,759.47	$30,766.19	$4,614.93	$538,921.02	$1,364,276.25
2036	78	$1,016,596.08	$20.30	$50,078.62	$0.16	$8,254.98	$41,823.64	$34,844.68	$5,226.70	$610,362.64	$1,443,971.42
2037	79	$1,024,508.50	$19.50	$52,538.90	$0.17	$8,767.89	$43,771.01	$39,248.02	$5,887.20	$687,494.46	$1,527,591.43
2038	80	$1,030,287.78	$18.70	$55,095.60	$0.17	$9,305.96	$45,789.64	$43,997.05	$6,599.56	$770,681.59	$1,615,517.57
2039	81	$1,033,703.70	$17.90	$57,748.81	$0.17	$9,869.42	$47,879.39	$49,113.66	$7,367.05	$860,307.59	$1,707,944.63
2040	82	$1,034,512.19	$17.10	$60,497.79	$0.17	$10,458.28	$50,039.51	$54,620.83	$8,193.12	$956,774.80	$1,805,074.80
2041	83	$1,032,455.26	$16.30	$63,340.81	$0.17	$11,072.30	$52,268.52	$60,542.60	$9,081.39	$1,060,504.53	$1,907,117.85
2042	84	$1,027,261.32	$15.50	$66,274.92	$0.18	$11,710.95	$54,563.97	$66,904.11	$10,035.62	$1,171,937.00	$2,014,291.28
2043	85	$1,018,645.58	$14.80	$68,827.40	$0.18	$12,270.35	$56,557.06	$73,709.64	$11,056.45	$1,291,147.25	$2,126,436.62
2044	86	$1,006,807.26	$14.10	$71,404.77	$0.18	$12,838.56	$58,566.21	$80,982.81	$12,147.42	$1,418,548.85	$2,244,130.80
2045	87	$991,526.64	$13.40	$73,994.53	$0.18	$13,412.69	$60,581.84	$88,747.84	$13,312.18	$1,554,566.35	$2,367,618.20
2046	88	$972,584.04	$12.70	$76,581.42	$0.18	$13,989.17	$62,592.25	$97,029.52	$14,554.43	$1,699,633.69	$2,497,152.60
2047	89	$949,762.78	$12.00	$79,146.90	$0.18	$14,563.67	$64,583.23	$105,853.02	$15,877.95	$1,854,191.98	$2,632,997.46
2048	90	$922,852.83	$11.40	$80,952.00	$0.18	$14,969.46	$65,982.54	$115,210.47	$17,281.57	$2,018,103.42	$2,774,842.75
2049	91	$892,414.88	$10.80	$82,631.01	$0.19	$15,348.02	$67,282.99	$125,123.18	$18,768.48	$2,191,741.12	$2,923,521.32
2050	92	$858,370.91	$10.20	$84,154.01	$0.19	$15,692.30	$68,461.72	$135,612.17	$20,341.83	$2,375,473.18	$3,079,337.32
2051	93	$820,669.91	$9.60	$85,486.45	$0.19	$15,994.17	$69,492.28	$146,697.93	$22,004.69	$2,569,658.70	$3,242,608.02
2052	94	$779,294.47	$9.10	$85,636.75	$0.19	$16,028.26	$69,608.50	$158,356.03	$23,753.40	$2,773,869.82	$3,412,891.29
2053	95	$735,277.18	$8.60	$85,497.35	$0.19	$15,996.64	$69,500.71	$170,602.23	$25,590.33	$2,988,382.43	$3,591,309.71
2054	96	$688,766.62	$8.10	$85,032.92	$0.19	$15,891.35	$69,141.57	$183,451.44	$27,517.72	$3,213,457.72	$3,778,246.35
2055	97	$639,957.73	$7.60	$84,204.96	$0.19	$15,703.83	$68,501.14	$196,917.53	$29,537.63	$3,449,338.76	$3,974,104.09
2056	98	$589,097.93	$7.10	$82,971.54	$0.19	$15,424.92	$67,546.61	$211,013.12	$31,651.97	$3,696,246.53	$4,179,306.83
2057	99	$536,493.97	$6.70	$80,073.73	$0.18	$14,771.87	$65,301.86	$225,692.90	$33,853.94	$3,953,387.36	$4,393,312.41
2058	100	$483,805.46	$6.30	$76,794.52	$0.18	$14,036.79	$62,757.73	$240,968.70	$36,145.31	$4,220,968.48	$4,617,688.96

Break even
5 Year periods

Option 2: Accelerated Conversion - Taxes paid from after tax dollars

Year	Age	Pre Tax Assets	Conversion Jan 1st	Effective Tax Rate	Less Taxes Jan 1st	Reinvested in Tax Free Roth	Profit	Tax Free Acct Total Dec 31st	Profit	Taxes on LTCG Dec 31st	Taxable Acct Total Per Year	Net Total combined
2018	60	$500,000.00	$85,000.00	$0.17	$14,516.39	$70,483.61	$4,229.02	$94,582.76	$4,409.02	$661.35	$77,231.27	$171,814.03
2019	61	$439,900.00	$85,000.00	$0.17	$14,516.39	$70,483.61	$4,229.02	$194,840.48	$3,762.89	$564.43	$65,913.34	$260,753.82
2020	62	$376,194.00	$85,000.00	$0.17	$14,516.39	$70,483.61	$4,229.02	$301,113.67	$3,083.82	$462.57	$54,018.19	$355,131.86
2021	63	$308,665.64	$85,000.00	$0.17	$14,516.39	$70,483.61	$4,229.02	$413,763.24	$2,370.11	$355.52	$41,516.39	$455,279.63
2022	64	$237,085.58	$85,000.00	$0.17	$14,516.39	$70,483.61	$4,229.02	$533,171.80	$1,620.00	$243.00	$28,376.99	$561,548.79
2023	65	$161,210.71	$85,000.00	$0.17	$14,516.39	$70,483.61	$4,229.02	$659,744.86	$831.64	$124.75	$14,567.49	$674,312.35
2024	66	$80,783.36	$80,783.36	$0.17	$13,691.93	$67,091.07	$4,025.46	$789,226.53	$52.53	$7.88	$920.22	$790,146.75
2025	67							$836,580.12	$55.21	$8.28	$967.15	$837,547.27
2026	68							$886,774.92	$58.03	$8.70	$1,016.48	$887,791.40
2027	69							$939,981.42	$60.99	$9.15	$1,068.32	$941,049.74
2028	70							$996,380.30	$64.10	$9.61	$1,122.80	$997,503.11
2029	71							$1,056,163.12	$67.37	$10.11	$1,180.06	$1,057,343.19
2030	72							$1,119,532.91	$70.80	$10.62	$1,240.25	$1,120,773.16
2031	73							$1,186,704.88	$74.41	$11.16	$1,303.50	$1,188,008.39
2032	74							$1,257,907.18	$78.21	$11.73	$1,369.98	$1,259,277.16
2033	75							$1,333,381.61	$82.20	$12.33	$1,439.85	$1,334,821.46
2034	76							$1,413,384.50	$86.39	$12.96	$1,513.28	$1,414,897.78
2035	77							$1,498,187.57	$90.80	$13.62	$1,590.46	$1,499,778.03
2036	78							$1,588,078.83	$95.43	$14.31	$1,671.57	$1,589,750.40
2037	79							$1,683,363.56	$100.29	$15.04	$1,756.82	$1,685,120.38
2038	80							$1,784,365.37	$105.41	$15.81	$1,846.42	$1,786,211.79
2039	81							$1,891,427.30	$110.79	$16.62	$1,940.59	$1,893,367.88
2040	82							$2,004,912.93	$116.44	$17.47	$2,039.56	$2,006,952.49
2041	83							$2,125,207.71	$122.37	$18.36	$2,143.57	$2,127,351.28
2042	84							$2,252,720.17	$128.61	$19.29	$2,252.90	$2,254,973.07
2043	85							$2,387,883.38	$135.17	$20.28	$2,367.79	$2,390,251.18
2044	86							$2,531,156.38	$142.07	$21.31	$2,488.55	$2,533,644.94
2045	87							$2,683,025.77	$149.31	$22.40	$2,615.47	$2,685,641.23
2046	88							$2,844,007.31	$156.93	$23.54	$2,748.86	$2,846,756.17
2047	89							$3,014,647.75	$164.93	$24.74	$2,889.05	$3,017,536.80
2048	90							$3,195,526.62	$173.34	$26.00	$3,036.39	$3,198,563.01
2049	91							$3,387,258.21	$182.18	$27.33	$3,191.24	$3,390,449.46
2050	92							$3,590,493.71	$191.47	$28.72	$3,354.00	$3,593,847.71
2051	93							$3,805,923.33	$201.24	$30.19	$3,525.05	$3,809,448.38
2052	94							$4,034,278.73	$211.50	$31.73	$3,704.83	$4,037,983.56
2053	95							$4,276,335.45	$222.29	$33.34	$3,893.78	$4,280,229.23
2054	96							$4,532,915.58	$233.63	$35.04	$4,092.36	$4,537,007.94
2055	97							$4,804,890.52	$245.54	$36.83	$4,301.07	$4,809,191.58
2056	98							$5,093,183.95	$258.06	$38.71	$4,520.42	$5,097,704.37
2057	99							$5,398,774.98	$271.23	$40.68	$4,750.97	$5,403,525.95
2058	100							$5,722,701.48	$285.06	$42.76	$4,993.26	$5,727,694.75

Break even

5 Year periods

Clearly, you can see how paying taxes now, when the tax rates are at historical lows, dramatically impact the long-term value of the investment using the Roth Window strategy.

Chapter 2 - Ninth wonder of the World

Albert Einstein has been credited with declaring **Compound Interest** as the eighth wonder of the world. We could not agree more. Gene has always been a saver, even as a child, squirreling money away in his piggy bank. Then, in Gene's freshman year in high school, in Mr. Mueller's accounting class, he first learned of compound interest and the phenomenon called *the time value of money*. He was hooked! Just as a snowball turns into an avalanche, saving and investing even the smallest amount of money could achieve significant wealth, given enough time. Time is the most important factor in developing wealth. From this one important lesson from a high school teacher, Gene was motivated to build enough wealth that he could live off the returns, having income for life, in perpetuity.

Enter the Roth. Gene believes the Roth savings retirement plan is the ninth wonder of the world, or at least it is in the United States. The Roth retirement savings plan, with the help of the time value of money, creates a vehicle that can provide tax-free growth for decades, even after you are gone. The Roth is not just a retirement savings plan. It is the best tax-free savings vehicle that can be used as a supplement to an emergency fund, college savings fund, or for any major purchase like a home or car. It can provide **non-taxable income** in retirement. Since distributions are not taxable income, you may qualify for low income tax credits, minimize taxes on Social Security, or reduced Medicare costs in retirement.

The Roth retirement savings plan can maximize your wealth and is the most underutilized estate planning tool available today, in the opinion of our resident financial wizard, Gene R. Ric. Keep in mind that every dollar you do not pay in taxes, is one more dollar in your pocket.

And again, examples are a great thing. Here we go with another one.

Example #2

As a graduation gift, Emily's grandfather deposited $5,500 into a Roth IRA when Emily graduated from college at age 25. When Emily reaches retirement age of 65, assuming a 6% rate of return, the Grandfather's gift would be worth $56,571.00. As most know, this is because that money is invested, making the original deposit get bigger, and later that larger amount continues to grow, and exponentially increases, year after year.

Following her grandfather's example, Emily has decided to contribute $5,500 every year thereafter, until she reaches the age of 65. Her retirement account will be worth $851,190 assuming a 6% rate of return.

Einstein was a smart fellow, wasn't he? Of course, that's been well documented.

Chapter 3 - The Benefits of a Roth IRA

A Roth can refer to an IRA (Individual Retirement Account) or an employer sponsored retirement account like a 401k, 403B or 401a. Let's discuss two concepts that are important to know about the Roth IRA: tax-free growth and withdrawals.

Tax-free Growth

A Roth retirement savings plan is funded with after-tax dollars, money that has already been taxed. This money grows over time, based on how it is invested. Let's put that in perspective. For all calculations in this book we have used a conservative rate of return of 6% as a way of eliminating investment rates from the conversation. The S&P 500 index, historically, over long periods of time, provide about a 10% rate of return. At a reasonable 7% rate of return your money doubles every 10.3 years. So, if you are 35 years old, with 30 years to retirement and $50,000 in your 401k, your money would double 3 time. $50,000 becomes $100,000, $100,000 become $200,000 and $200,000 becomes $400,000. This is a very simple example, but the point is that given enough time and patience, anyone can be a millionaire. The trick is to start young, make consistent contributions, and to patient. It is never a profit or loss until you sell.

Having your money in a Roth eliminates taxes from the equation. Roth assets provide the flexibility to manipulate your income in retirement.

Withdraws

Money that you contribute to a Roth IRA can be withdrawn at any time without paying additional taxes or incurring financial penalties. Although the purpose of the Roth is to provide tax-free growth for retirement savings, the added benefit of being able to withdraw contributions without penalty provides an added cushion during periods of hardship.

Example #3

Bradley is 35 years old and has $18,000 in a savings account that serves as his emergency fund. Many financial experts suggest such an emergency fund should consist of enough cash to cover three to six months of essential expenses, and so for Bradley, he's got about $3,000 of essential expenses per month for six months, or in other words, $18,000. He has been contributing the maximum $5,500 to a Roth IRA for the last 10 years. His Roth is currently worth $72,500 based on a 6% rate of return. Since Bradly can withdraw up to $55,000 with no taxes or penalties, he decides to reduce his emergency fund by half and supplement it with his Roth Contributions in the event he has an emergency. The excess funds from the reduced emergency fund can be invested to provide greater wealth or help with larger purchases like a car or down payment for a home.

Required Minimum Distribution (RMD)

Tax payers that have pre-tax retirement savings accounts, (401k's, 403B's or a Traditional or Rollover IRA) are required to begin withdrawing money from their pre-tax account in the year of reaching the age of 70½. Required Minimum Distributions (RMDs) are calculated using the uniform life tax table which is a life expectancy divisor. For example, the first divisor is 27.4. You would divide your December 31st pre-tax account balance of the prior year, by the divisor. Conventional thinking suggests you will be in a lower tax bracket in retirement than when you are working. This is why advisors recommend a pre-tax contribution over a Roth between the ages of 50 and 65. The truth is that if you have, or are projected to have, more than a million dollars in pre-tax assets by the time you reach the age to 70½, you may be in a higher tax bracket while in retirement, depending on your social security and other income, when you start to take RMDs and current tax rates will have expired (by 2025).

In addition to paying income tax on your RMDs as the funds are withdrawn, those monies are no longer benefiting from a tax advantaged account. If reinvested in a taxable brokerage account, you will now be responsible for taxes on long-term and short-term capital gains, dividends and interest on those investments.

A Roth IRA does not require RMDs so the hard-earned cash you put into one of these accounts can stay in a tax advantaged state through the end of your days. As we consider time value of money, the additional time spent in the Roth tax-free growth account can have even greater benefits. Now consider this: not only do the assets grow tax-free for your lifetime, but they also grow tax-free for the lifetime of your heirs that receive the funds. The beneficiary will have to take RMDs from the Inherited Roth IRA, but it is a non-taxable event. Think of the power we've discussed about the time value of money and its impact on your assets with 50 years of tax-free growth! If the plan is followed, a typical, middle class American could create wealth that can be handed down from generation to generation.

Chapter 4 – Funding of a Roth

There are two primary ways of funding a Roth:

- Contributions
- Conversions

It is important to understand the difference and the limitations of each, and your strategies to maximize both funding methods.

Contributions

The IRS limits contributions for both pre-tax and after-tax IRA accounts to $5,500. This amount increases to $6,500 if you are over the age of 50. For the conversations in this book, we'll assume you are not over 50 and focus on this amount being $5,500.

There are income limits and phase-outs for making contributions to a Roth IRA which we will discuss shortly. Ideally, contributions are preferred as they have the added advantage of being withdrawn at any time, tax-free, penalty free.

If you're not familiar with the world of investing, you may not realize how important it is to consider if the money you put into the IRA is "after-tax," meaning it has already been taxed (i.e., income from your paycheck has already been dinged by Uncle Sam), or if it is "pre-tax," meaning it has not yet been taxed (i.e., Uncle Sam will be expecting you to pay up at some point in the future). How you use after-tax and pre-tax money can have an important impact on the amount of taxes you pay over your lifetime.

A key element of the Roth Window Strategy is to get as much money as possible into a Roth before 2026. Using after-tax contributions to a Roth IRA helps you start with more money, and build more money, more quickly. For example, if you make the maximum after-tax contribution of $5,500, ALL that money can go into a Roth. If you make the same $5,500 contribution into a pre-tax Traditional IRA, that money will be taxed when withdrawn, so in today's dollars, it is more like $4,400 actual dollars. Yes, we could also talk about the pros and cons of getting taxed now or later, and that's a relevant discussion, but our key point here and now, is that using after-tax contributions gets more money into your Roth so it can start growing into a larger mountain of money down the road.

To be able to make contributions to an IRA, you must have earned income. Earned income includes:

- wages
- salaries
- tips
- professional fees
- bonuses
- other amounts received for providing personal services
- commissions
- self-employed income
- alimony and maintenance payments

Earned income does not include:

- earnings and profit from property, such as rental income, interest income, or dividend income
- pension and annuity income
- deferred compensation
- disability income
- unemployment compensation
- child support

Something else you need to know about contributions is that it's quite possible you might make too damn much money for the government's liking, which can knock you out of the Roth game, or limit how much you can invest.

Source: Internal Revenue Service

Backdoor Roth IRA

If you are *not* eligible to contribute directly to a Roth IRA due to your adjusted gross income being too marvelously high, never fear, there is still a strategy for funding a Roth IRA. It is commonly referred to as the **backdoor method**. There is no income limitation to contributing to a Traditional IRA. The income limitation for Traditional IRA's is for the ability to deduct the contribution from your income on your tax return. **There is no income limitation** to simply contributing to a Traditional IRA.

The backdoor funding of a Roth IRA is accomplished by a contribution to a Traditional IRA with after-tax dollars, and then a few days later (as soon as the money is fully collected), do a Roth Conversion. This will allow you to convert $5,500 per year ($6,500 if over age 50) to a Roth IRA. It can take time to build your snowball, but worth it in the end. We encourage you to consult with a tax advisor to determine if a form 8606 is required to ensure basis is report properly to the IRS.

Warning! If you have any traditional IRAs with pre-tax dollars, the IRS will look at the conversion proportionately to the total of all pre-tax IRA's that you have, creating a taxable event. What does this really mean? It means the IRS will look beyond just the money you are putting into the IRA for doing a Backdoor Roth, they will look at your larger portfolio of IRA accounts only to see if they can collect some taxes there because of what you are doing here. Does that make sense? Maybe we need an example.

Example #4

James can no longer take tax deductions in a Traditional IRA because he makes too damn much money. He can, however, make contributions to the

Traditional IRA. Ultimately, what James really wants to do is to put retirement money into a Roth, but he can't make contributions directly because, again, he makes too damn much money. However, since he can make contributions to the Traditional IRA, he can use that as a tool to get his money into a Roth, using the Backdoor Roth technique we talked about above.

To do this, let's say James will make a $5,000 nondeductible contribution to a Traditional IRA and then convert the funds to a Roth a few days later. Now, this seems straightforward, but there's something else James needs to know. The IRS knows he also happens to have $10,000 sitting in a separate Traditional pre-tax IRA. That IRA is *not* involved in his funding of the Roth, so why do we bring this up? Because, the IRS looks at **all** of James's pre-tax IRAs (traditional or rollover) during the taxable year that he's doing this backdoor maneuver, and they will look to tax the sum of all his IRA investments, proportionately.

So, our man James wants to get $5,000 into the Roth via the backdoor, and he already has $10,000 sitting in another traditional IRA, so that makes a total of $15,000 that the IRS will scrutinize. One-third of that total is after-tax dollars in the backdoor maneuver, the other two-thirds is sitting in that other traditional IRA as pre-tax dollars. Thus, the IRS sees that two-thirds of that $15,000 could be taxed, so they will tax two-thirds of his $5,000 conversion during that tax year. This is what we mean by "proportionately" as mentioned earlier. In terms of dollars, this means he'll claim about $3,333.50 of the conversion as taxable income.

James has a few clever options to protect his money as best as he can.

1. He can roll his pre-tax IRA assets into an active employer 401k plan, assuming they accept the assets, prior to making the contribution for purpose of a backdoor Roth. This way, the IRS won't look at his whole portfolio as a means of collecting taxes, like in our example. He won't have pre-tax dollars sitting in a pre-tax traditional IRA, and the IRS will leave that $10,000 unmolested.

2. He could make the conversion and pay the taxes. And, keep in mind, under the current tax rates that are the result of 2018 legislation, current rates are more favorable than prior to 2018. Also keep in mind, that the important thing is that he's getting money into the Roth, which will help him build wealth over time, more efficiently than keeping his money in the traditional IRA. So, this isn't exactly a horrible thing to do… to pay taxes. Sometimes you just gotta pay da man, as they say.

3. There's one more option James could take, but we'll address it in detail, later. Instead of contributing using the backdoor approach, he could do a conversion instead of a contribution. Remember, contributions and conversions are two distinctly different approaches for funding a Roth IRA. And, luckily for you, the reader, you don't have to wait very long to read about this… it's the next chapter!

Chapter 5 - Conversions

There are two primary ways to fund a Roth IRA. We have discussed contributions and the relatively low amounts of money you can contribute into the Roth per year. The second method of funding a Roth is by conversion. It is important to understand the difference. A conversion is simply taking pre-tax dollars and converting them to after-tax Roth dollars by paying the income taxes on these dollars in the year in which you convert the funds. (A conversion may also be after-tax, discussed later). Note, if you are under the age of 59½, there is no penalty associated with a Roth conversion. These pre-tax dollars could be in a Traditional IRA, a Rollover IRA, an employer sponsored 401k or 403b, or could come from a lump sum distribution from a pension plan. These types of retirement plan generally have far more pre-tax dollars due to the higher contribution limits for employer plans $18,500 ($24,000 over 50), plus an employer match. There is no limit to the amount of money that you can convert into a Roth. When converting, you do want to keep in mind how a large conversion can impact your total tax situation, however.

Chapter 6 - Restrictions of a Roth

We have discussed funding, now let's cover withdraws. A Roth has two 5-year aging periods that are used to impose restrictions to withdrawing your money.

Five-year aging period #1

The first aging period is from the time you first open your very first Roth, if you withdraw any **earnings** out of the account prior to meeting the five-year aging period, you may be subject to a 10% penalty plus taxes. As true with both pre-tax retirement and Roth accounts, withdraws under the age of 59½ are subject to a 10% penalty. There are some waivers of this penalty so do your homework.

Five-year aging period #2

The second five-year aging period for a Roth involves conversions. Every time you make a Roth conversion, a new five-year aging period starts on the earnings that accumulate from that conversion. If you are under the age of 59½, the 10% penalty may also apply to the converted amount.

Roth IRA Distributions

Categories of money in a Roth IRA

Classification / Reason for Withdraw	Contributions (3)			Conversions / per conversion (3)				Earnings (3)			
	Prior to satisfying the 5 year aging (1)		After satisfying the 5 year aging (1)		Prior to satisfying 5 year holding period (2)		After satisfying 5 year holding period (2)		Prior to satisfying (1)		After satisfying 5 year aging (1)	
	Taxable	10% Penalty	Taxable	10% penalty	Taxable	10% penalty	Taxable	10% penalty	Taxable	10% penalty	Taxable	10% penalty
Before 59.5 (No Exception)	No	No	No	No	No	Yes	No	No	Yes	Yes	Yes	Yes
After 59.5 (QD)	No	No	No	No	No	No	No	No	Yes	No	No (QD)	No (QD)
Death (QD)	No	No	No	No	No	No	No	No	Yes	No	No (QD)	No (QD)
Disability (QD)	No	No	No	No	No	No	No	No	Yes	No	No (QD)	No (QD)
1st Home Purchase (QD)	No	No	No	No	No	No	No	No	Yes	No	No (QD)	No (QD)
401k QDRO (QD)	No	No	No	No	No	No	No	No	Yes	No	No (QD)	No (QD)
401k Rule 55 (QD)	No	No	No	No	No	No	No	No	Yes	No	No (QD)	No (QD)
Before 59.5 Exceptions												
SEPP / 72-T	No	No	No	No	No	No	No	No	Yes	No	Yes	No
Medical Exp >10% AGI	No	No	No	No	No	No	No	No	Yes	No	Yes	No
Health Ins Prem Unemployed	No	No	No	No	No	No	No	No	Yes	No	Yes	No
Higher Education	No	No	No	No	No	No	No	No	Yes	No	Yes	No
IRS Tax Levy	No	No	No	No	No	No	No	No	Yes	No	Yes	No

1 The Five Year Aging Beginnings January 1st or the year which the first contribution is made.
2 The Holding Periods start on January 1st of the year of the conversion.
3 Order money is distributed FIFO (first in, first out), 1st- contributions, 2nd- taxed conversions, 3rd- non-taxed conversions, 4th- Earnings

Withdraws

Money that you contribute to a Roth IRA can be withdrawn at any time without any taxes or penalties. Although the purpose of the Roth is to provide tax-free growth for retirement savings, the added benefit of being able to withdraw money without taxes or penalty provides an added cushion during periods of hardship. Remember Example #3?

Once you have met the aging periods and obtained age 59½, all withdraws from a Roth are tax-free and penalty free, but still must be reported on your tax return. This ability to withdraw non-taxable income gives you incredible control. By layering your Roth non-taxable dollars and your pre-tax retirement dollars, you can control which tax bracket you are in each year in retirement. This affects the amount of taxes you pay on your social security income as well and Medicare benefits.

Required Minimum Distribution (RMD)

As discussed in Chapter 3, tax payers that have pre-tax retirement savings accounts, (401k's, 403B's or a traditional or rollover IRA) are required to begin withdrawing money from their pre-tax account in the year of reaching the age of 70½. The IRS will require you to start taking money out of your retirement savings plan, whether you want to or not. Failure to take an RMD may result in a 50% penalty of your RMD. Ouch! You might as well take an unplanned cruise rather than kiss half of your money goodbye! By requiring you to remove the money over time, you are paying taxes and generating tax revenue for the IRS. This continues until you have paid taxes on all your pre-tax retirement savings or you die. If you die, your beneficiaries will be responsible for paying those taxes until all pre-tax money has been removed from the pre-tax retirement accounts.

In addition to paying income tax on your RMDs as the funds are withdrawn, those monies are no longer benefiting from a tax advantaged account. If reinvested in a taxable brokerage account, you will now be responsible for taxes on long-term and short-term capital gains, dividends and interest on those investments.

A Roth IRA is not subject to RMDs, so these monies can stay in a tax advantaged account for the life of the individual owner. Note that an employer plan, 401k, 403b, and 401a do require RMDs on Roth assets. As we consider the time value of money, the additional time spent in the Roth with tax-free growth can have a significant benefit.

Now consider this: not only do the assets grow tax-free for your lifetime, but they also grow tax-free for the lifetime of your heirs that receive the funds. The beneficiary will have to take RMDs from the inherited Roth IRA, but it is a non-taxable event. Think of the power of time value of money on your assets with 50 years of tax-free growth! If the plan is followed, the average middle-class family could create wealth that can be handed down from generation to generation.

Employer Sponsored 401k, 401a, and 403b, Retirement Saving Plans

Employer sponsored retirement savings plans are governed by the Department of Labor, set in place by ERISA (Employee Retirement Income Security Act) of 1974. These types of retirement savings plans are the building blocks of retirement income and savings. These plans, in today's landscape, are generally defined contribution plans that include a 401k feature, which means the employees elect to contribute a portion of their salary toward their retirement. It may be supplemented with a match from the employer and provide an opportunity to contribute more than three times the amount of money you can contribute to an IRA, which are governed by the IRS (Internal Revenue Service).

Employer plans allow employees the option to direct up to $18,500 of their income into a retirement savings plan. In the year you turn 50, you can begin contributing an additional $6,000 catch up contribution, for a total of $24,500 per year. Traditionally these deferrals where pre-tax, so the employee was able to reduce their reported earned income thereby reducing income tax. The pre-tax dollars would benefit from tax deferred growth, meaning you would be responsible for income tax upon withdraw in retirement. In 2006 Congress authorized the use of Roth retirement savings plans within a 401k under the Internal Revenue Code (IRC 402a). Since that time, employers have adopted the Roth as an option within their retirement savings plan. Note that the employers match is always pre-tax and there is a tax incentive for them to provide this benefit.

It is important to understand that every employer plan is uniquely different. There are some common guidelines governing employer retirement saving plans under the Department of Labor. Many of the qualifying rules put in place were designed to prevent highly compensated employees/executives from abusing these plans. If you have a Financial Advisor, he or she may not have knowledge of your unique plan and the benefits available to you. Consult with your plan custodian to learn about the unique features of your retirement savings plan.

With the introduction of the Roth into employer plans, also came the ability to convert already existing pre-tax balances in your 401k to Roth after-tax dollars called a Roth In-Plan Conversion. Not every employer plan will provide this option. The alternative would be to roll your pre-tax retirement savings (401K, 403B, 401A) to a Rollover IRA (Individual Retirement Account) and convert your pre-tax dollars to Roth after-tax dollars, outside of your employer plan, assuming you have withdrawal options available.

After-Tax Contributions

ATTENTION HIGHLY COMPENSATED EMPLOYEES — if you earn more income than you need to meet your essential and discretionary needs, there may be an opportunity to contribute even more money toward retirement savings via after-tax contributions. The important thing to understand about after-tax monies is that they can later be converted to a Roth IRA (or Roth through an in-plan conversion if your employer allows) as a non-taxable transaction. Remember, if these funds are not converted, all earnings are taxable. There are limits on the total amount of retirement contributions that can be made in a given year. These contribution limits were designed to prevent the abuse of tax deferred vehicles by highly compensated employees. The maximum total contribution by employee and employer combined in 2018 is $55,000 plus the $6,000 of catch-up if you are over the age of 50. So, let's assume you are 55 years old and contribute the $18,500 maximum allowed contribution to a pre-tax or Roth employer plan. Your employer provides a percentage match, for a maximum of an additional $7,000. In total, you have $25,500 of benefit. You could contribute an addition $29,500 in after-tax contributions taking you up to the maximum $55,000 limit, Plus the additional $6000 of catch-up you are eligible to contribute because you are over the age of 50 which can be Roth or pre-tax. You potentially can contribute $61,000 into a tax advantaged retirement savings account per year. Keep in mind that you can contribute to both an employer plan (401K, 403B, 401A) and an IRA. One does not prevent the other. So, you would add an additional $6,500, over age 50, of IRA contributions using the backdoor Roth funding method for a total annual tax advantaged savings of $67,500 per year.

This strategy assumes you are the highest tax brackets. It may be beneficial to make your $18,500 and $6,000 catch up contribution as pre-tax, reducing your taxable income. This assume you will be in a lower tax bracket in retirement. The after-tax is going to be taxed at your current rate no matter what. This strategy gives you the option to convert the funds into a tax-free state, a Roth IRA. The Roth Window favors middle and upper middle-income taxpayers. When you are in the highest tax brackets the current tax rates begin to even out. Your effective tax rate may still be lower. This becomes a personal decision based on your unique circumstances. Did we mention you should always consult with a tax advisor? You may need to file a form 8606 to insure the after-tax dollars are not viewed as taxable by the IRS.

Example #6

Jerome is 30 years old, he works in the technology industry. He is single with no debt and minimal financial needs. He makes $185,000 per year. He is comfortable living on $90,000 per year. His employer provides a 401k that offers the ability to contribute to a Roth and the employer matches a maximum of $5,000. Jerome could contribute the minimum to receive the employers match, which would leave him with excess income that he could put into a taxable brokerage account. The other option would be to contribute the maximum of $18,500 to his Roth 401k. He would receive his employers full match of $5,000. Rather than receive taxed income that would go into his brokerage account, Jerome decides to increase his after-tax contributions allowed by his employer plan. This allows him to contribute an additional $31,500 of after-tax money into his employer plan per year ($55,000-($18,500+$5,000)=$31,500). As Jerome contributes money to the after-tax source within his plan, he rolls the money out of his employer plan, as a conversion, to a Roth IRA once a quarter. Rather than build a balance in the after-tax account which is subject to long term and short-term capital gains, dividends and interest, Jerome's money grows tax-free. Remember, he is 30 years old. If he contributes an extra $25,000 per year in after-tax money and then converts it to a Roth IRA, assuming a 6% rate of return, Jerome would have $919,640 in tax-free money in his Roth IRA through after-tax conversions by the time he is 50 years old. Add in the $680,500 in his Roth 401k and the $183,900 of pre-tax 401k assets from his employer match, and We would say Jerome could consider early retirement!

Chapter 7 – Paying Taxes

When converting pre-tax dollars to Roth after-tax dollars, you will need to be prepared to pay the taxes on the additional income reported in that tax year. The best strategy is to pay the taxes with after-tax dollars from a savings/brokerage account or from current income. The other option would be to pay the taxes from the pre-tax dollars. This is highly discouraged if you are under the age of 59½ as the taxes would be viewed as a withdraw, and subject to taxes and penalties. If you do pay taxes out of the pre-tax account and you are between the ages of 59 ½ and 70, you will reach a breakeven point around 12 to 15 years down the road under current tax rates.

If you are of RMD age or will be of RMD age before 2025 when the rates expire, you could use your RMD to pay the taxes. This would only make sense as an estate planning strategy for your heirs to benefit from tax-free growth. The conversion strategy is far more profitable if you can pay taxes from a taxable brokerage account or savings under current tax rates.

When considering a conversion to take advantage of the Roth Window, the first step would be to consider your total pre-tax assets and the amount you want to convert each year for the next eight years. The goal is not to convert all your funds as quickly as possible. An additional feature of the Tax Cuts & Jobs Act of 2018 is the doubling of the standard deduction ($12,000 single, $24,000 married filing Joint). This is especially beneficial for older tax payers that might not have mortgage interest as an itemized deduction under 2017 tax rules. By spreading out your conversion over all eight years, you are ensuring that you are taking full advantage of the standard deduction, further lowering your taxable income and effective tax rate. This increased standard deduction will also expire December 31st, 2025. It is recommended you consult a tax advisor to determine the amount to convert, and whether you will need to make estimated quarterly tax payments to avoid penalties. Be aware of the tax bracket you may be in with the additional income from the conversion and how the total income can affect other aspects of your unique tax situation.

Investments

Now that you have funded your Roth, it is important that you are invested properly. Throughout this book, and in the models, we have used a 6% rate of return as a constant, to remove investment performance as a variable in the modeling of this strategy. A 6% rate of return is a conservative rate of return in a balanced portfolio that contains exposure to diversified stock holdings. As you look at your entire portfolio, the maximum portion of your stock portfolio should be in the Roth to take advantage of the tax-free growth the Roth provides.

Example #7

Let's say you have a $5,000,000 of net worth at age 65. You decide that your allocation should be 50% stocks, 40% bonds and 10% cash and your investable assets are in a pre-tax 401k, a Roth IRA and a brokerage account. Below is an example of how your total investable assets might be proportioned to maximize the tax-free growth of a Roth.

Account Type	Assets	Allocation
401k	$3,000,000	16% cash / 17% stock / 67% bonds
Roth IRA	$1,500,000	100% stock
Brokerage / Savings Account	$500,000	100% stock

(investment income tax rates are generally lower than Income tax rate)

Note that the Roth is 100% stocks. This allows you to maximize the tax-free growth.

Chapter 8 - Thank You, President Trump

Love him or hate him, he has provided the greatest tax reform bill we have seen in decades. The Roth Window suggests an eight-year window of opportunity to position pre-tax assets into a tax-free state for decades to come. Carpe diem: "Seize the Day."

This strategy is based on the existing and new tax reform currently in place. Things can change at any moment and this strategy could quickly become mute. There are no guarantees in life or taxes. Your decision to pursue this strategy is purely yours, with the knowledge that nothing lasts forever.

Adjusted Individual Tax Brackets and Lower Rates

The new tax code has reduced several of the marginal income tax rates (see chart below). More importantly, note the increased thresholds for the new tax brackets. This is key in providing a lower effective tax rate for large conversions. There are several other changes to the individual tax code. My goal, and the foundation of the Roth Window, is **TIME**. Many of the changes in the Tax Cuts & Jobs Act of 2018 could all be temporary — Congress would need to extend the period or the rules would revert back to 2017 tax rates after December 31, 2025.

SINGLE TAXPAYERS

2018 Tax Rates – Standard Deduction $12,000		2017 Tax Rates – Standard Deduction $6,350	
10%	0 to $9,525	10%	0 to $9,325
12%	$9,525 to $38,700	15%	$9,325 to $37,950
22%	$38,700 to $82,500	25%	$37,950 to $91,900
24%	$82,500 to $157,500	28%	$91,900 to $191,650
32%	$157,500 to $200,000	33%	$191,650 to $416,700
35%	$200,000 to $500,000	35%	$416,700 to $418,400
37%	Over $500,000	39.60%	Over $418,400

MARRIED FILING JOINTLY & SURVIVING SPOUSES

2018 Tax Rates – Standard Deduction $24,000		2017 Tax Rates – Standard Deduction $12,700	
10%	0 to $19,050	10%	0 to $18,650
12%	$19,050 to $77,400	15%	$18,650 to $75,900
22%	$77,400 to $165,000	25%	$75,900 to $153,100
24%	$165,000 to $315,000	28%	$153,100 to $233,350
32%	$315,000 to $400,000	33%	$233,350 to $416,700
35%	$400,000 to $600,000	35%	$416,700 to $470,700
37%	Over $600,000	39.60%	Over $470,700

The Tax Cut & Jobs Act of 2018 is the heart of the Roth Window strategy. The window being the window of opportunity that presents itself until the window closes.

We have provided some examples of the strategy but have also run several different scenarios. The key takeaways are:

- The best use of the strategy is to pay taxes on the conversion out of an after-tax savings/brokerage account. This has a two-fold benefit. It is moving your pre-tax retirement savings to a tax-free growth state. It is also moving your investments in an after-tax brokerage account to a tax-free growth state, free of investment income tax on long-term and short-term capital gains, dividends and interest. Under this method, assuming conversion is complete prior to December 25th, 2025, our modeling suggests a five-to-six years breakeven point. Any profit beyond 6 years is tax-free and adds to your wealth.

- If you don't have the after-tax dollars in a savings/brokerage account to pay the taxes and you can't pay them out of ordinary income, you could pay the taxes with the pre-tax dollars during the conversion. This is highly discouraged if you are under 59½ as this would be subject to taxes and penalties. But if you are over 59 ½ and do pay taxes out of the conversion, the breakeven is closer to 12 years to recover the taxes and rebuild the reduction in tax-advantaged dollars.

Chapter 9 - Warning Will Robinson, Warning!

The Roth Window strategy is suggesting the accelerated conversion of pre-tax dollars to take advantage of lower effective tax yields before they expire December 25, 2025. Any time we have increased income it is important to understand how this additional income can affect our total tax picture.

Income Thresholds to Be Aware of

Medicare Surtax

There is an additional Medicare surtax of 3.8% on net investment income plus capital gains taxes that came into play as part of the Affordable Care Act. This tax may be triggered when your MAGI is greater than, $200,000 filing single, $250,000 married filing jointly. So ideally you would not want to convert an amount that would push your total income above these limits if you have a significant after-tax brokerage account. This also serves as an additional incentive to use your taxable investment assets to pay the tax on conversion, reducing your taxable investment account.

Medicare Part B

If you are age 63, or will be before 2025, your income may affect Medicare Part B costs. You will pay the least amount for Medicare Part B when your income is less than $85,000 with a look back period of two years. So, if you are 63 years of age or older, and on Medicare, you need to evaluate if this strategy makes sense.

Let's say you have converted a large amount of money into a Roth and you are in retirement. Distributions from a Roth are non-taxable, which means that you can withdraw as much as you wish to live on, but if you keep your reported income below $85,000, you are saving on Medicare Part B as a bonus to the Roth Window strategy.

College Credits

There are other tax credits and deductions that may be jeopardized by reporting higher income. If you have children of college age, or will be of college age, before 2025, you may want to limit your conversions, and by extension, your reported Modified Adjusted Gross Income (MAGI). Generally, the more money you make, the less you'll receive in student loan assistance.

Note that a parent's retirement assets like an IRA, Roth, or 401k do not count against a student when filing for FAFSA (Free Application for Federal Student Aid). A 529 is considered the student's assets and can affect FAFSA (some private schools do consider a parent's retirement assets).

American Opportunity Tax Credit

This provides a dollar for dollar tax credit, 100%, on your tax return for the first $2,000 you pay for qualified education expenses and 25% credit for the next $2,000. This tax credit can only be used for four years and is per child. It is important to know the requirements and phase out of this credit. If your MAGI married filing joint is greater than $160,000 the benefit will phase out between $160,000 and $180,000. The range for filing single is $80,000 to $90,000. So, when determining the amount of pre-tax dollars to convert, be aware of these thresholds.

Lifetime Learning Credit

This provides a tax credit of 20% up to $10,000, per family for tuition and fees. The threshold for married filing jointly is $112,000 to $132,000, single is $56,000 to $66,000. You will need to determine which is more important to you, the tax credit or the conversion.

Things to Consider Prior to Converting

There are a few situations to consider prior to converting pre-tax dollars to a Roth. One involves highly appreciated employer stock in an employer sponsored retirement savings plan. There is tax strategy called **Net Unrealized Appreciation** (NUA) which allows you to separate employer stock from an employer sponsored retirement savings plan and place the stock in an after-tax brokerage account. This may allow you the opportunity to pay lower investment income tax rates on any profit that has accumulated in the retirement savings plan rather than the pay higher income tax rates at the time of withdraw. If you have highly appreciated employer stock in an employer sponsored retirement savings plan, contact a tax advisor to determine if you qualify and if it makes sense for you to consider NUA as a tax strategy. Note that there are qualifying events that make NUA available. If you take a withdraw from your account prior to considering NUA as an option, you may forfeit this strategy, so contact a tax adviser first before taking any action.

Another consideration is whether you plan to be charitable with your assets in retirement and at end of life. If you have pre-tax assets that you intend to donate, it may be better for you, and the receiving institution, to donate pre-tax assets rather than pay the taxes on the assets to convert to Roth and then donate. From an IRA, if you are 70½ or older and taking RMDs, you can make a **Qualified Charitable Donation** where the donation can be made directly to the charity. You pay no taxes and the distribution satisfies your RMD.

Also, be aware of state taxes in the state in which you currently live vs. where you plan to retire. We have not accounted for states with high income tax rates. If you live is a state with high income tax rates, like California, AND plan to retire and move to a state with lower or no income taxes, like Texas or Florida, there may be justification for a pre-tax retirement savings account over a Roth. We believe this is a small percentage of the whole, but again, consult with a tax advisor to determine what strategies work best for you.

Chapter 10 - Welcome to Retirement

To this point, we have discussed the benefits of Roth assets, the Roth Window of opportunity that exists, the different methods of funding a Roth, the qualifications that must be met before withdrawing earnings and some limitations when determining how much to convert. Let's fast forward 15 to 20 years from now. You are retired and have cash flow from social security to meet essential expenses and a few other sources. You can enjoy a comfortable retirement by drawing as much money as you choose from your Roth assets. These withdraws do not count toward your MAGI. Having the flexibility to control your income provides additional opportunities to control taxes paid on social security, reduce health care costs, and potentially take advantage of additional credit.

Earlier we discussed Medicare Part B and to be aware of how conversions that are reported can increase your income and affect your costs once on Medicare. Now in retirement, you can control your reported income to minimize your Medicare Part B costs.

And Then You Die

There are a few key themes that drive this strategy and why it can be so impactful. First is the time value of money, by far the most important. The more time money must compound, the more wealth, or income from investments, you will have. Second is the Roth itself, *The Ninth Wonder of the World*, providing the ability for your money to grow free of taxes, with no requirement to remove the money from the shelter of the Roth or taxes on any growth that you experience up until you pass.

When your assets are inherited, the beneficiary will be required to take out RMDs from the Roth account. These distributions are not taxable, but it does force out the funds eventually, so they no longer enjoy tax-free growth, unless of course your heirs use the RMD to make contributions into their own Roth IRA. If you have significant financial assets, we would suggest a gifting strategy of making Roth contributions on behalf of your children, or grandchildren. Consider it a Christmas gift that has a built-in penalty for early withdraw. This extends the lifetime of your asset's tax-free growth. It addresses the five-year aging of a Roth while they are young. There is also a unique opportunity to avoid taxes and penalties on earnings for first time home purchase. Remember, this is how a snowball becomes an avalanche for decades to come. Always keep significant assets to provide for extended health care needs for you and your spouse. You can gift up to $14,000 per year, per person, without triggering any form of gift tax. The maximum Roth contribution is $5,500 ($6,500 if they are over the age of 50). Keep in mind the person you are gifting to must have earned income. We also see it as an opportunity to test the waters. Legally the money is theirs and they can take out the contribution without penalty. Give them the instructions the money is not to be touched, hopefully it will become an avalanche. If they access the funds without permission, and they demonstrate an incapacity to handle money and the problems it can create, then you could put on the parenting hat one more time, stop making the contributions and consider the need for a Trust account to control inheritance after you kick the bucket.

Lessons Learned

We have run several scenarios. For those is higher income tax brackets, north of $200,000 in annual income, the benefit of the Roth Window begins to fade. The difference in tax rates between 2018 and the future rates in 2025, diminish the benefit of the Roth Window. If you are a high-income earner, conventional wisdom may apply, and you may be better off taking the tax cut now by making pre-tax contribution and consider Roth conversion once in retirement. That said, we did provide the after-tax strategy that may be available in your employer retirement savings plan. You could make you pre-tax contributions up to $18,500 and then contribute to your After-tax source, converting After tax source to a Roth. There is no down side to this strategy. The alternative option is to pay the taxes and invest in an after-tax brokerage account, subject to long-term, short-term capital gains, dividend and interest.

Roth vs. Pre-tax Retirement Savings Plans

We touched on this briefly in the beginning of this book but let us revisit. Ask any advisor which is better, a traditional IRA or a Roth IRA, and most will tell you it depends on your circumstances. There can be short term tax strategies that may favor one over the other in any given year. We are in for the long haul, to build as much wealth as possible. We believe the Roth is the better choice. Certainly now, and for the next 8 years, we believe that the Roth presents the greatest opportunity for tax-free living.

Beyond 2025, we believe if long term generational wealth is your goal, the Roth is still the better choice.

First, a Roth provides tax-free growth and tax-free withdrawals which give you control over your reported taxable income in retirement.

Second, since there are no RMDs from a Roth for the owner, your assets potentially have decades of additional time to grow tax-free. For the rest of your life time and the life time of your loved ones.

Third, a Roth after-tax dollar is a whole dollar, all 100 pennies. There is a concept called Net Neutrality that suggest there is no difference between a pre-tax retirement contribution and an after-tax Roth contribution. If you contribute $100.00 to a pre-tax Traditional IRA, and it grows for 20 years at 6%, you would have $320.71. If we then tax that amount at 20% upon withdraw, you would have $256.57. Now let's consider an after-tax Roth contribution. The $100.00 is taxed upfront leaving you $80.00 to be invested at 6%. After 20 years you have $256.57. So, the net is the same. The problem with this example is that IRA's/401k's do not have a pre-tax contribution limit and an After-tax contribution limit. For a Roth IRA, if you make a $5,500 maximum contribution, it is the whole $5,500. After 20 years a 6% you would have $17,639.25 of tax-free money. If we make the same maximum $5,500 contribution into a Traditional IRA, it will also be worth $17,639.25 at the end of 20 years, but it then needs to be taxed at

20% upon withdraw for a net of $14,111.40. So, you see, these dollars are not equal and if your goal is to maximize your generational wealth, the Roth is the better choice.

For these three reasons, we believe the Roth is the best choice for building generational wealth. Again, the ninth wonder!

In Closing

We hope you have found some value in this strategy. There is far more information available regarding retirement planning, IRAs, and employer sponsored savings plans. We have only addressed the issues that directly involve Roths and the conversion of pre-tax dollars. We encourage everyone to consult with a tax advisor, financial planner, custodians of your employer plan, or do your own homework. There are great resources to help you be successful.

And may your money survive you, to bless your descendants for decades to come!

www.ingramcontent.com/pod-product-compliance
Lightning Source LLC
Chambersburg PA
CBHW070959240526
45469CB00017B/2486